The Scottish Collection

Scottish
VERSE

SELECTED BY
JAMES CARNEY

HarperCollins*Publishers*

HarperCollins Publishers
PO Box, Glasgow G4 0NB

First published 1998

Reprint 10 9 8 7 6 5 4 3 2 1 0

© HarperCollins Publishers, 1998 (this selection)

ISBN 0 00 472166 7

A catalogue record for this book is available from the British Library

Printed and bound in Italy by Rotolito Lombarda S.p.A., Pioltello

Contents

Acknowledgments

The Publishers would like to thank the following for their kind permission to reproduce material in this book:

John Murray (Publishers) Ltd for *The Finished House* and *Horse* by George Mackay Brown

Carcanet Press Ltd for *Strawberries* by Edwin Morgan

Glasgow Museums and Art Galleries for *Girl on a Bicycle* by Joseph Crawhall (p.36); *Highland Mary and Robert Burns* by Thomas Faed (p.39); *The Last of the Clan* by Thomas Faed (p.52); *Two Strings to her Bow* by John Pettie (p.56)

Lord Semphill for *Glasgow Exhibition 1888* by Sir John Lavery (p.15)

United Distillers Art Collection for *The Thin Red Line* by Robert Gibb (p.19); *Ties That Bind* by Jack Vettriano (p.35); *The Highland Whisky Still* by Sir Edwin Landseer (p.59)

The Carson Clark Galleries, Edinburgh for the 1745 map of Scotland by R.W. Seale (p.51)

The National Trust for Scotland for *Blue Flax* by E.A. Hornel (p.60)

Robert Fleming & Co. Ltd for *Robert the Bruce and De Bohun* by Eric Harald Macbeth Robertson (p.20); *Girl with Fruit* by Dorothy Johnstone (p.40)

Regimental HQ Kings' Own Scottish Borderers for *Killiecrankie* (p. 28)

Mirror Syndication International for the photograph of the recovery of the Stone of Destiny in Arbroath Abbey, 1950 (p.23)

Historic Scotland for the photograph of the 'Honours of Scotland' (p.27)

The photographs on pp. 7, 8, 11, 12, 24, 44, 48, and 53 were taken by Keith Allardyce (© HarperCollins) and on p.31 by James Carney

In the finished house, a flame is brought to the hearth.
Then a table, between door and window
Where a stranger will eat before the men of the house.
A bed is laid in a secret corner
For the three agonies – love, birth, death –
That are made beautiful with ceremony.
The neighbours come with gifts –
A set of cups, a calendar, some chairs,
A fiddle is hung on the wall.
A girl puts lucky salt in a dish.
The cupboard has its loaf and bottle.
On the seventh morning
One spills water of blessing over the threshold.

I saw a stranger yestreen;
I put food in the eating place;
Drink in the drinking place;
Music in the listening place;
In the sacred name of the Triune;
He blessed myself and my house;
My cattle and my dear ones;
And the lark said in her song,
  Often, often, often
Goes the Christ in the stranger's guise,
  Often, often, often
Goes the Christ in the stranger's guise

From the island of Eigg

Here's a bottle and an honest friend
  What wad ye wish for mair, man?
Wha kens, before his life may end,
  What his share may be o' care, man?

Then catch the moments as they fly,
  And use them as ye ought, man;
Believe me, happiness is shy,
  And comes no ay when sought, man!

An I mo chridhe, I mo gràidh
An àit' guth manaich bidh geum bà;
Ach mu'n tig an Saoghal gu crìch
Bithidh I mar a bha.

In Iona of my heart, Iona of my love
Instead of monks' voices shall be lowing of cattle;
But ere the world shall come to an end
Iona shall be as it was.

O, beautiful city of Glasgow, which stands on
    the river Clyde.
How happy should the people be which in ye reside:
Because it is the most enterprising city of the present
    day.
Whatever anybody else may say.

The ships which lie at the Broomielaw are
    most beautiful to see,
They are bigger and better than any in Dundee;
Likewise the municipal buildings, most gorgeous to be
    seen,
Near to Ingram Street, not far from Glasgow Green.

O, wonderful city of Glasgow, with your triple
    expansion engines,
At the making of which your workmen get many
    singeins;
Also the deepening of the Clyde, most marvellous to
    behold,
Which cost much money, be it told.

Then there is a grand picture gallery,
Which the keepers thereof are paid a very large salary;
Therefore, citizens of Glasgow, do not fret or worry,
For there is nothing like it in Edinburgh.

O, beautiful city of Glasgow, I must conclude my lay,
By calling thee the greatest city of the present day:
For your treatment of me was by no means churlish,
Therefore, I say, "Let Glasgow Flourish."

And wasna he a roguey,
A roguey, a roguey,
And wasna he a roguey,
The piper o' Dundee?

The piper came to our town,
To our town, to our town,
The piper came to our town,
    And he played bonnilie.
He played a spring the laird to please,
A spring brent new frae yont the seas;
And then he ga'e his bags a wheeze,
    And played anither key.

He played *The welcome owre the main*,
And *Ye'se be fou and I'se be fain*,
And *Auld Stuarts back again*,
    Wi' muckle mirth and glee.
He played *The Kirk*, he played *The Quier*,
The Mullin Dhu and *Chevalier*,
And *Lang awa', but welcome here*,
    Sae sweet, sae bonnilie.

It's some gat swords, and some gat nane,
And some were dancing mad their lane,
And mony a vow o' weir was ta'en
    That night at Amulrie!
There was Tullibardine and Burleigh,
And Struan, Keith, and Ogilvie,
And brave Carnegie, wha but he,
    The piper o' Dundee?

Here's to it!
The fighting sheen of it,
The yellow, the green of it,
The white, the blue of it,
The swing, the hue of it,
The dark, the red of it,
Every thread of it!

The fair have sighed for it,
The brave have died for it,
Foemen sought for it,
Heroes fought for it,
Honour the name of it,
Drink to the fame of it –

THE TARTAN!

Scots, wha hae wi' Wallace bled,
Scots, wham Bruce has aften led,
Welcome to your gory bed
              Or to victorie!

Now's the day, and now's the hour:
See the front o' battle lour,
See approach proud Edward's power –
              Chains and slaverie!

Wha will be a traitor knave?
Wha can fill a coward's grave?
Wha sae base as be a slave? –
              Let him turn, and flee!

Wha for Scotland's King and Law
Freedom's sword will strongly draw,
Freeman stand, or freeman fa',
              Let him follow me!

By Oppression's woes and pains,
By your sons in servile chains,
We will drain our dearest veins
              But they shall be free!

Lay the proud usurpers low!
Tyrants fall in every foe!
Liberty's in every blow! ·
              Let us do, or die!

The Wee Magic Stane — John McEvoy

Oh the Dean o' Westminster wis a powerful man.
He held a' the strings o' the state in his hand.
But with all this great business it flustered him nane,
Till some rogues ran away wi' his wee magic stane,
Wi' a too - ra - li - oor - a - li - oor - a - li - ay.

Noo the stane had great pow'rs that could dae such a thin'
And withoot it , it seemed, we'd be wantin' a king,
So he called in the polis and gave this degree–
"Go an' hunt oot the Stane and return it tae me."

So the polis went beetlin' up tae the North
They huntit the Clyde and they huntit the Forth
But the wild folk up yonder jist kiddit them a'
Fur they didnae believe it was magic at a'.

Noo the Provost o' Glesca, Sir Victor by name,
Was awfy pit oot when he heard o' the Stane
So he offered the statues that staun' in the Square
That the high churches' masons might mak a few mair.

When the Dean o' Westminster wi' this was acquaint,
He sent fur Sir Victor and made him a saint,
"Now it's no use you sending your statues down heah"
Said the Dean "but you've given me a jolly good ideah."

So he quarried a stane o' the very same stuff
An' he dressed it a' up till it looked like enough
Then he sent for the Press and announced that the Stane
Had been found and returned to Westminster again.

When the reivers found oot what Westminster had done,
They went aboot diggin' up stanes by the ton
And fur each wan they feenished they entered a claim
That this was the true and original stane.

22

Noo the cream o' the joke still remains tae be tellt,
Fur the bloke that was turnin' them aff on the belt
At the peak o' production was so sorely pressed
That the real yin got bunged in alang wi' the rest.

So if ever ye come on a stane wi' a ring
Jist sit yersel' doon and appoint yersel King
Fur there's nane wud be able to challenge yir claim
That ye'd croont yersel King on the Destiny Stane.

March, march, Ettrick and Teviotdale,
    Why the deil dinna ye march forward in order?
March, march, Eskdale and Liddesdale,
All the Blue Bonnets are bound for the Border.
        Many a banner spread
        Flutters above your head,
    Many a crest that is famous in story.
        Mount and make ready then,
        Sons of the mountain glen,
    Fight for the Queen and the old Scottish glory.

Come from the hills where your hirsels are grazing,
Come from the glen of the buck and the roe;
Come to the crag where the beacon is blazing,
Come with the buckler, the lance, and the bow.
        Trumpets are sounding,
        War-steeds are bounding,
    Stand to your arms then, and march in good order;
        England shall many a day
        Tell of the bloody fray,
    When the Blue Bonnets came over the Border.

Fareweel to a' our Scottish fame,
Fareweel our ancient glory!
Fareweel ev'n to the Scottish name,
Sae famed in martial story!
Now Sark rins over Solway sands,
An' Tweed rins to the ocean,
To mark where England's province stands–
Such a parcel of rogues in a nation!

What force or guile could not subdue
Thro' many warlike ages
Is wrought now by a coward few
For hireling traitor's wages.
The English steel we could disdain,
Secure in valour's station;
But English gold has been our bane–
Such a parcel of rogues in a nation!

O, would, or I had seen the day
That Treason thus could sell us,
My auld grey head had lien in clay
Wi' Bruce and loyal Wallace!
But pith and power, till my last hour
I'll mak this declaration:–
'We're bought and sold for English gold'–
Such a parcel of rogues in a nation!

Whaur hae ye been sae braw lad?
Whaur hae ye been sae cantie-o?
Whaur hae ye been sae braw lad?
Cam' ye by Killiecrankie-o?

And ye had been whaur I hae been,
Ye wadna been sae cantie-o
And ye had seen what I hae seen
On the braes o' Killiecrankie-o

I fought at land, I fought at sea
At hame I fought my auntie-o
But I met the Devil and Dundee
On the braes o' Killiecrankie-o

The bold Pictur fell wi' a fur
And Clavers gat a clankie-o
And I had fed an Atholl gled
On the braes of Killiecrankie-o

O fie, Mckay, what gart ye lie
In the bush ayont the brankie-o
Ye'd better kissed King Willie's loof
Than come by Killiecrankie-o

There's nae shame, there's nae shame
There's nae shame tae swankie-o
There's soor slaes on Atholl's braes
And the De'il at Killiecrankie-o

Bonnie Charlie's noo awa,
    Safely o'er the friendly main;
Mony a heart will break in twa,
    Should he ne'er come back again.

Will ye no come back again?
Will ye no come back again?
Better lo'ed ye canna be.
Will ye no come back again?

Ye trusted in your Hieland men,
    They trusted you, dear Charlie!
They kent your hiding in the glen,
    Death and exile braving.

English bribes were a' in vain,
    Tho' puir and puirer we maun be;
Siller canna buy the heart
    That aye beats warm for thine and thee.

We watched thee in the gloamin' hour,
    We watched thee in the mornin' grey;
Though thirty thousand pounds they gie,
    Oh, there is nane that wad betray!

Sweet's the laverock's note, and lang,
    Liltin' wildly up the glen;
But aye to me he sings ae sang,
    "Will ye no come back again?"

Will ye no come back again?
Will ye no come back again?
Better lo'ed ye canna be.
Will ye no come back again?

I've heard them lilting at our yowe-milking–
    Lasses a-lilting before dawn of day;
But now they are moaning on ilka green loaning–
    The Flowers of the Forest are a' wede away.

At buchts, in the morning, nae blythe lads are scorning;
    Lasses are lonely, and dowie and wae; –
Nae daffin', nae gabbin' but sighing and sabbing
    Ilk ane lifts her leglin and hies her away.

In hairst, at the shearing, nae youths now are jeering–
    Bandsters are runkled and lyart or grey:
At fair or at preaching, nae wooing, nae fleeching:
    The Flowers of the Forest are a' wede away.

At e'en, in the gloaming, nae swankies are roaming,
    'Bout stacks with the lasses at bogle to play;
But ilke ane sits drearie, lamenting her dearie–
    The Flowers of the Forest are a' wede away.

Dool and wae for the order sent our lads to the Border!
    The English, for ance, by guile wan the day;–
The Flowers of the Forest, that foucht aye the foremost–
    The prime o' our land–are cauld in the clay.

We'll hear nae mair lilting at the yowe-milking;
    Women and bairns are heartless and wae,
Sighing and moaning on ilka green loaning–
    The Flowers of the Forest are a' wede away.

My dear and only Love, I pray
 This noble World of thee,
Be govern'd by no other Sway
 But purest Monarchie.
For if Confusion have a Part,
 Which vertuous Souls abhore,
And hold a Synod in thy Heart,
 I'll never love thee more.

Like *Alexander* I will reign,
 And I will reign alone,
My Thoughts shall evermore disdain
 A Rival on my Throne.
He either fears his Fate too much,
 Or his Deserts are small,
That puts it not unto the Touch,
 To win or lose it all.

But if thou wilt be faithful then,
 And constant of thy word;
I'll make thee glorious by my pen
 And famous by my sword,
I'll serve thee in such noble ways
 Were never heard before!
I'll crown and deck thee with all bays
 And love thee evermore.

Jenny kiss'd me when we met,
    Jumping from the chair she sat in;
Time, you thief, who love to get
    Sweets into your list, put that in!
Say I'm weary, say I'm sad,
    Say that health and wealth have miss'd me,
Say I'm growing old, but add,
    Jenny kiss'd me.

Jenny Kiss'd Me

Leigh Hunt

Ae Fond Kiss
Robert Burns

Ae fond kiss, and then we sever,–
Ae fareweel, and then – for ever
Deep in heart-wrung tears I'll pledge thee!
Warring sighs and groans I'll wage thee!

Who shall say that fortune grieves him,
While the star of hope she leaves him?
Me, nae chearfu' twinkle lights me,–
Dark despair around benights me.

I'll ne'er blame my partial fancy,
Naething could resist my Nancy;
But to see her, was to love her–
Love but her, and love for ever.

Had we never lov'd sae kindly–
Had we never lov'd sae blindly–
Never met – or never parted,
We had ne'er been broken-hearted!

Fare-thee-weel, thou first and fairest!
Fare-thee-weel, thou best and dearest!
Thine be ilka joy and treasure,
Peace, Enjoyment, Love and Pleasure!

Ae fond kiss, and then we sever!
Ae fareweel, alas! for ever!
Deep in heart-wrung tears I'll pledge thee!
Warring sighs and groans I'll wage thee!

There were never strawberries
like the ones we had
that sultry afternoon
sitting on the step
of the open french window
facing each other
your knees held in mine
the blue plates in our laps
the strawberries glistening
in the hot sunlight
we dipped them in sugar
looking at each other
not hurrying the feast
for one to come
the empty plates
laid on the stone together
with the two forks crossed
and I bent towards you
sweet in that air
in my arms
abandoned like a child
from your eager mouth
the taste of strawberries
in my memory
lean back again
let me love you
let the sun beat
on our forgetfulness
one hour of all
the heat intense
and summer lightning
on the Kilpatrick hills

let the storm wash the plates

This ae nighte, this ae nighte,
Every nighte and alle,
Fire, and sleet, and candle-lighte;
And Christe receive thye saule.

When thou from hence away art paste,
Every nighte and alle,
To Whinny-muir thou comest at laste;
And Christe receive thye saule.

If ever thou gavest hosen and shoon,
Every nighte and alle,
Sit thee down and put them on;
And Christe receive thye saule.

If hosen and shoon thou ne'er gavest nane,
Every nighte and alle,
The whinnes sall pricke thee to the bare bane
And Christe receive thye saule.

From Whinny-muir when thou mayst passe,
Every nighte and alle,
To Brig o' Dread thou comest at laste;
And Christe receive thye saule.

From Brig o' Dread when thou mayst passe,
Every nighte and alle,
To purgatory fire thou comest at laste;
And Christe receive thye saule.

If ever thou gavest meate or drinke,
Every nighte and alle,
The fire sall never make thee shrinke:
And Christe receive thye saule.

If meate or drinke thou gavest nane,
  Every nighte and alle,
The fire will burn thee to the bare bane;
  And Christe receive thye saule.

This ae nighte, this ae nighte,
  Every nighte and alle,
Fire, and sleet, and candle-lighte;
  And Christe receive thye saule.

Here lies interr'd a man o' micht,
  They ca'd him Malcolm Downie;
He lost his life ae market nicht,
  By fa'ing aff his pownie.
                    Aged 37 years.

Andrew Meekie, late Parish Dominie

Beneath this stanes lye MEEKIE'S banes
O Sawtan, gin ye tak him
Appeynt him tutor to your weans
An' clever deils he'll mak 'em

                    1696

Here lies Mass. Andrew Gray
Of whom ne muckle good can I say
He was ne Quaker, for he had ne spirit
He was ne Papist, for he had ne merit
He was ne Turk, for he drank muckle wine
He was ne Jew, for he eat muckle swine
Full forty years he preach'd and le'ed
For which God doom'd him when he de'ed

    Here lys
    James Stewart
    He sall rys

…The wind blew as 'twad blawn its last;
The rattling showers rose on the blast;
The speedy gleams the darkness swallow'd;
Loud, deep, and lang the thunder bellow'd:
That night, a child might understand,
The Deil had business on his hand.

Weel mounted on his gray mare Meg,
A better never lifted leg,
Tam skelpit on thro' dub and mire,
Despising wind, and rain, and fire;
Whiles holding fast his guid blue bonnet,
Whiles crooning o'er some auld Scots sonnet,

Whiles glow'ring round wi' prudent cares,
Lest bogles catch him unawares:
Kirk-Alloway was drawing nigh,
Whare ghaists and houlets nightly cry.

The doubling storm roars thro' the woods;
The lightnings flash from pole to pole;
Near and more near the thunders roll:
When, glimmering thro' the groaning trees,
Kirk-Alloway seem'd in a bleeze,
Thro' ilka bore the beams were glancing,
And loud resounded mirth and dancing.

And, wow! Tam saw an unco sight!
Warlocks and witches in a dance:
Nae cotillion, brent new frae France,
But hornpipes, jigs, strathspeys, and reels,
Put life and mettle in their heels.

A winnock-bunker in the east,
There sat Auld Nick, in shape o' beast;
A tousie tyke, black, grim and large,
To gie them music was his charge:
He screw'd the pipes and gart them skirl,
Till roof and rafters a' did dirl.
Coffins stood round, like open presses,
That shaw'd the dead in their last dresses;
And, by some devilish cantraip sleight,
Each in its cauld hand held a light:
By which heroic Tam was able
To note upon that haly table,
A murderer's banes, in gibbet-airns;
Twa span-lang, wee, unchristen'd bairns;
A thief new-cutted frae a rape—
Wi' his last gasp his gab did gape;
Five tomahawks wi' bluid red-rusted;
Five scimitars wi' murder crusted;
A garter which a babe had strangled;
A knife a father's throat had mangled—
Whom his ain son o' life bereft—
The grey hairs yet stack to the heft;
Wi' mair o' horrible and awfu',
Which even to name wad be unlawfu'.
Three lawyers' tongues, turned inside out,
Wi' lies seamed like a beggar's clout;
Three Priests' hearts, rotten, black as muck,
Lay stinking, vile, in every neuk…

The Lord maist hie
I know will be
An herd to me;
I cannot lang have stress, nor stand in neid;
He makes my lair
In fields maist fair,
Quhair I bot care,
Reposing at my pleasure, safety feid.
He sweetly me convoys,
Quhair naething me annoys,
But pleasure brings.
He brings my mynd
Fit to sic kynd,
That foes, or fears of foe cannot me grieve.
He does me leid
In perfect freid,
And for his name he never will me lieve.
Thoch I wald stray,
Ilk day by day,
In deidly way,
Yet will I not dispair; I fear none ill,
For quhy thy grace
In every place,
Does me embrace,
Thy rod and shepherd's crook me comfort still.
In spite of foes
My tabil grows,
Thou balms my head with joy;
My cup owerflows.
Kyndness and grace,
Mercy and peice,
Sall follow me for all my wretched days,
And me convoy,
To endless joy,
In heaven quhair I sall be with thee always

49

Breathes there the man with soul so dead,
Who never to himself hath said,
"This is my own, my native land!"
Whose heart hath ne'er within him burn'd
As home his footsteps he hath turn'd
From wandering on a foreign strand?
If such there breathe, go, mark him well;
For him no Minstrel raptures swell;
High though his titles, proud his name,
Boundless his wealth as wish can claim;
Despite those titles, power, and pelf,
The wretch, concentred all in self,
Living, shall forefeit fair renown,
And, doubly dying, shall go down
To the vile dust from whence he sprung,
Unwept, unhonour'd, and unsung.

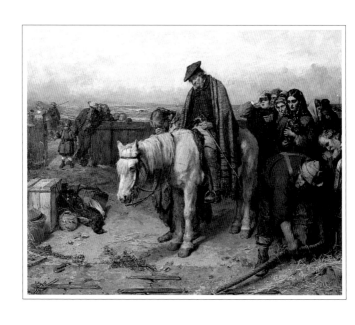

Blows the wind to-day, and the sun
  and the rain are flying,
    Blows the wind on the moors to-day and now,
Where about the graves of the martyrs
  the whaups are crying,
    My heart remembers how!

Grey recumbent tombs of the dead in desert places,
    Standing stones on the vacant wine-red moor,
Hills of sheep, and the howes of the silent
  vanquished races,
    And winds, austere and pure;

Be it granted me to behold you again in dying,
    Hills of home! and to hear again the call;
Hear about the graves of the martyrs the pee-wees crying,
    And hear no more at all.

In Exile

Robert Louis Stevenson

The horse at the shore
Casks of red apples, skull, a barrel of rum

The horse in the field
Plough, ploughman, gulls, a furrow, a cornstalk

The horse in the peat-bog
Twelve baskets of dark fire

The horse at the pier
Letters, bread, paraffin, one passenger, papers

The horse at the show
Ribbons, raffia, high bright hooves

The horse in the meadow
A stallion, a red wind, between the hills

The horse at the burn
Quenching a long flame in the throat

So, we'll go no more a roving
  So late into the night,
Though the heart be still as loving,
  And the moon be still as bright.

For the sword outwears its sheath,
  And the soul wears out the breast,
And the heart must pause to breathe,
  And love itself have rest.

Though the night was made for loving,
  And the day returns too soon,
Yet we'll go no more a roving,
  By the light of the moon.

The Deil's awa, the Deil's awa,
*   The Deil's awa wi' th' Exciseman!*
He's danced awa, he's danced awa,
*   He's danced awa wi' th' Exciseman!*

The Deil cam fiddlin through the town,
    And danc'd awa wi' th' Exciseman,
And ilka wife cries:– 'Auld Mahoun,
    I wish you luck o' the prize, man!

We'll mak our maut, and we'll brew our drink,
    We'll laugh, sing, and rejoice, man,
And monie braw thanks to the meikle black Deil,
    That danc'd awa wi' th' Exciseman.

There's threesome reels, there's foursome reels,
    There's hornpipes and strathspeys, man,
but the ae best dance ere cam to the land
    Was *The Deil's Awa wi' th' Exciseman*

/

Should auld acquaintance be forgot,
And never brought to mind?
Should auld acquaintance be forgot,
And auld lang syne?

For auld lang syne, my dear,
For auld lang syne,
We'll tak a cup o' kindness yet
For auld lang syne!

And surely you'll be your pint-stoup,
And surely I'll be mine;
And we'll tak a cup o' kindness yet
For auld lang syne!

We twa hae run about the braes,
And pu'd the gowans fine;
But we've wander'd mony a weary fit
Sin auld lang syne.

We twa hae paidl'd in the burn,
Frae morning sun till dine;
But seas between us braid hae roar'd
Sin auld lang syne!

And there's a hand, my trusty fiere,
And gie's a hand o' thine;
And we'll tak a right gude-willie waught,
For auld lang syne.

Auld Lang Syne

Robert Burns

Glossary

Rune of Hospitality
yestreen: yesterday   Triune: the Holy Trinity

A Bottle and a Friend
mair: more   wha: who   kens: knows

The Piper o' Dundee
spring: a lively dance   brent: brought   frae yont: from over
ga'e: gave   muckle: great   sae: so   gat: got   mony: many
weir: war   their lane: on their own

Scots Wha Hae
wha hae: who have   wham: whom   aften: often   lour: threaten

Blue Bonnets over the Border
hirsel: a flock of sheep

Killiecrankie
cantie: lively   gat a clankie: took a heavy blow   gled: a horesefly
or cleg   ayont: beyond   loof: palm of the hand

Will Ye No Come Back Again?
kent: knew   siller: silver, i.e. money   gloaming: evening twilight
laverock: skylark

The Flowers of the Forest
lilting: singing quietly   yowe: ewe   ilka: every   loaning: common
pasture   wede away: carried off, i.e. dead   buchts: sheepfolds
blythe: cheery   clowie: drooping   wae: sad   daffin: having fun
gabbin: chatting   sabbing: sobbing   ilk: each   leglin: milk pail
hairst: harvest   bandsters: a harvester who binds the sheaves
runkled: wrinkled, i.e. old   lyart: white-haired

fleeching: flattering, i.e. chatting up   e'en: evening
gloaming: evening twilight   swankies: smart young men
bogle: hide-and-seek   ilke: each   dool: mourning   ance: once
wan: won

Grave Humour
dominie: school teacher   Sawtan: Satan   gin: if   appeynt: appoint
deils: devils

Tam o' Shanter
skelpit: moved quickly   dub: puddles   bogles: hobgoblins   ghaists:
ghosts   houlets: owls   bleeze: ablaze   bore: small hole   cotillion:
a Continental dance   winnock-bunker: window seat   Auld Nick:
the Devil   tousie tyke: rough-haired mongrel   gart: made   dirl:
ring   presses: cupboards   cantrap sleight: magic spell   haly table:
altar   span-lang: newborn   gab: mouth   heft: handle   clout:
clothes   neuk: corner

The Deil's Awa wi' th' Exciseman
Exciseman: Government tax-collector   Auld Mahoun: the Devil
ilka: every   maut: malted barley   monie: many   meikle: large

Auld Lang Syne
auld lang syne: times long past   you'll be: you'll pay for   pint-stoup:
a four-pint measure   gowan: wild daisy   mony a weary fit: many
tired steps, i.e. a great distance   sin: since   paidl'd: paddled
braid: broad   fiere: friend   gie's: give me   gude-willie waught: a
good-will drink

COLLINS

Other titles in *The Scottish Collection* series are:

Scottish Recipes
ISBN 0 00 472167 5
£4.99

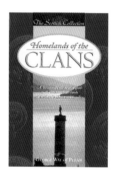

Homelands of the Clans
ISBN 0 00 472165 9
£4.99

Classic Malts
ISBN 0 00 472068 7
£4.99